Women in Treatment:

Creating a New Self-Image

About the author:

Barbara McFarland, Ed.D., is a psychologist in private practice. She is the clinical consultant for a number of alcoholism treatment programs in Ohio including Eden Treatment Center for Women, Inc., a women's residential treatment program. She has been active in providing treatment services to women through initiating all-female aftercare and treatment groups and providing seminars and workshops for the alcoholic woman. Her experience in working at male/female treatment programs has prompted her to develop the strategies in this manual.

Women in Treatment:

Creating a New Self-Image

by Barbara McFarland, Ed.D.

First published January, 1984.

ISBN: 0-89486-196-4

Printed in the United States of America.

Editor's Note:
Hazelden Educational Materials offers a variety of information on chemical dependency and related areas. Our publications do not necessarily represent Hazelden or its programs, nor do they officially speak for any Twelve Step organization.

CONTENTS

APPENDIXES

FOREWORD

This manual is an attempt to provide effective and comprehensive treatment to alcoholic women. It is not a complete treatment curriculum, but a unit of group strategies directed specifically at women patients. These groups are intended to supplement any core treatment program. Because of their disease, and other cultural hindrances, women have yet to reach their full potential as human beings. We as therapists and alcoholism counselors have a responsibility to help women believe in themselves.

"It can't be true!" gasped yellow. "How can I believe there's a butterfly inside you or me when all I see is a fuzzy worm? How does one become a butterfly?" she asked pensively.

"You must want to fly so much that you are willing to give up being a caterpillar."

"You mean to *die?*" asked yellow, remembering the three who fell out of the sky.

"Yes and no," he answered. "What *looks* like you will die, but what's *really* you will still live. Life is changed, not taken away. Isn't that different from those who die without ever becoming butterflies?"

HOPE FOR THE FLOWERS by Trina Paulus
© 1972 by Trina Paulus. Used by permission of Paulist Press.

INTRODUCTION

Despite the strides the women's movement has made in the last two decades, double standards still exist. The phrase "double standard" usually implies standards of a sexual nature, but there is another, less obvious, double standard that deals with alcohol. The underlying message for both is the same: good girls don't drink or enjoy sex, bad girls do.

Historically, women have been debased for drunkenness, which is often associated with sexual misconduct. Women who use alcohol to excess are often viewed as unscrupulous and corrupt. Women who are stricken with the disease of alcoholism, whose major symptom is uncontrollable use of the drug, are not exempt from this stigma.

Although science has yet to isolate the physiological cause of alcoholism, it has been recognized as a chronic, progressive, and fatal disease. Although stressful conditions do not create alcoholism, they certainly contribute to its escalation, and can affect the quality of the recovery process.

For women, a primary stressor is their perceived powerlessness and second class status in our society. For centuries, the female had been responsible for major tasks related to the survival of the family. The traditional productive skills of women—making clothing, canning, cooking—were a major source of pre-industrial woman's dignity and self-esteem. Before industrialization, she was viewed as an integral and equal contributor to the overall functioning of the family. With the advance of technology, her major "jobs" were moved into the marketplace, leaving her with the sole responsibility of caring for family and home. Although these are vital skills, they are not marketable commodities. The work world places little value on her contributions; consequently, she is not perceived as important. Even when she does move into the marketplace, she still earns only about fifty-nine cents to the man's dollar. The cultural message is quite clear: "You are not as important as your male counterpart." With this state of economic affairs, a woman is made to feel that she needs someone else in order to survive. This cultural labeling of "Man, the Breadwinner," and "Woman, the Tender of the Hearth," has placed the female on a pedestal. Drunkenness is an abdication of this primary role and a threat to the moral and social ideals that women have represented in our society.

Women have been taught to strive for perfection in their role as wives and mothers: to put everyone else first, to be self-sacrificing. Growing up, a little girl is encouraged to please her parents and teachers. She is rewarded for her passivity and compliance. When she marries, she works very hard at pleasing her husband, her in-laws, and then her children. Having the smartest kids, the most successful husband, the cleanest house, and baking the best cookies are her priorities. And if she works, either by choice or because of financial necessity, then she has to do all of the above in addition to being the perfect employee. The pressure is intense. She is often able to achieve her self-esteem only in relation to others, something that perpetuates her helplessness.

Not measuring up, making a mistake of any kind, no matter how trivial, is often interpreted as failure. When husband, children, parents, in-laws, or employer aren't pleased with her, or with her behavior, she internalizes this as HER failure.

Not being able to handle it all may push her into depression. The feelings of failure in such a case are so painful, her self-esteem so low, that she may inadvertently turn to something to numb it all. Some turn to food, sex, work, or alcohol.

For the woman who turns to drink, the drug initially gives her a false sense of power, strength, courage, and sexuality. For a while, she can do it all. She has sudden bursts of energy. However, frequent drinking awakens a sleeping giant and many of the following things may happen. The very thing she hoped drinking would help begins to haunt her. Criticism from significant others (husband, children, parents, employer) only perpetuates her self-hate. She plunges deeper into the bottle.

Her drinking contributes to the neglect of her responsibilities, making her more helpless and dependent. She blames herself rather than the alcohol for this state of affairs. The effects of the drug are such that her reality, emotions, and perceptions are all greatly distorted. Her self-esteem withers.

Finally, if she is lucky enough to get into treatment, she enters with shame and a deep sense of embarrassment. What she usually discovers after a short while is that she is not such a bad person after all. She works hard at fitting easily into the structure of the program and usually does well in the eyes of the staff and her peers. The knowledge she acquires at a cognitive level is invaluable. The sense of shame and guilt is temporarily lifted because she has learned that she has a disease and is not a villainous or immoral person.

However, those psychological issues unique to the female are not dealt with. The myths that a female alcoholic may try to perpetuate in treatment go something like this:

"No one ever saw me drunk."
"No one really knew I was drinking."
"I only drank when my husband did."
"My kids were always taken care of before I drank."
"I did my drinking when everyone was in bed."
"I never drank in a bar."
"Once I stop drinking, everything will be back to
   normal."

She has to protect her "pedestal" position. Although the staff may confront her on these issues, they don't often help her work through the feelings that underlie the female myth: powerlessness, anger/rage, helplessness, guilt. Her culturally learned people-pleasing skills get her to acknowledge staff confrontations but they rarely break through the myth. Staff and peers may unintentionally feed the myth because they are unaware of their own sex biases, which work to perpetuate her feelings of inadequacy as a female.

Once she graduates and returns home, post-treatment euphoria usually fades and the pressures of the family resume. Her significant others begin to expect her to return to her normal duties now that she is not drinking. They expect her to fit into the mold of caretaker and nurturer and to get back up on that pedestal. They often resent her involvement in Alcoholics Anonymous and aftercare groups because they feel that this takes time that belongs to them. The recovering woman begins to feel a real female conflict: "Do I behave selfishly and go to A.A. or do I put my family first?"

The old feelings of failure, depression, anger, and impotence begin to surface. The fear of losing the approval of those she loves puts her in a bind. She can't do what she needs to do to stay sober for fear of losing those she depends on; she can't continue recovering without displeasing them.

The pats on the back that she received in treatment fade into meaninglessness, and now she views herself as a person with a disease who is a failure. She just can't get back up on that pedestal, and she wonders what is wrong with her. If she could get back up there, someone will take care of her. Nothing frightens her more than having to take care of herself.

So, once again, she may be dry, but she hasn't touched on those psychological issues that can truly put her on the road to quality recovery. She must see that her position on the pedestal keeps her a second class citizen and subject to binds which give rise to these feelings of inadequacy. This is a major obstacle to recovery.

TREATMENT ISSUES
FOR WOMEN

Treatment programs have been developed primarily with the male in mind. Despite the fact that the disease is the same for both men and women, there are critical recovery and treatment issues that are quite different.

I. Dependency Issues

Trapped within economic and emotional dependencies, a woman's primary relationships are skewed because she occupies a powerless position. Rather than behaving in an active and instrumental way, articulating her needs and trying to get those needs met, she allows those whom she perceives as powerful to set up rules for her behavior. This increases her feelings of helplessness and impotence. The female alcoholic is especially susceptible to this because by turning over the power, she protects her habit. As long as she can get someone to take care of her, she is free to drink and use drugs.

In treatment, therefore, a woman must explore how she functions in relationships. Before she can begin to take responsibility for her life, she must learn how she perpetuates dependencies and how she allows others to define and control her. Although the payoffs of a childlike existence of safety and security seem numerous at the outset of the relationship, she must come to realize how they stifle her personal growth and development.

She must develop a belief in her feelings and learn to assert herself appropriately. This is contingent on the self-esteem she possesses. She has to believe in her own strength before she can believe in her capacity to take care of herself.

II. Depression

Chemically dependent women experience depression with much greater intensity because of the effects of the chemical on their central nervous system. In general, women as a population report experiencing depression at a higher rate than men. The literature suggests that this is due in large part to the feelings of impotence women experience in their own lives.

Women often feel overwhelmed by their environment because they have not been taught to use their own resources to cope with these feelings. They generally look to someone they perceive as powerful—either a man or a strong woman—to make them feel better. Because this is impossible, they often feel disappointed and assume that they weren't good enough to get that good feeling from outside themselves.

In addition to feelings of powerlessness and inadequacy, repressed anger and rage also contribute to a woman's depression. Women have been taught that it is not ladylike to be angry, that they should always be pleasant and agreeable. A woman should sacrifice her needs for those of her partner or children; and her payoff will be that she will be taken care of, emotionally and economically. When this doesn't happen, and in most cases it doesn't because it is totally unrealistic, she becomes enraged, feeling cheated and used. However, she cannot express these feelings for fear of losing the relationship.

Treatment groups should educate women about depression, and how to cope with it through their own inner resources.

III. Sexual Issues

Sexual abuse, promiscuity, rape, and frigidity are sexual experiences which many alcoholic women have had. Because of the shame and embarrassment they feel, they do not often discuss these issues, especially in a mixed group.

The double standard of sex is equivalent in many ways to the double standard of alcoholism. This attitude forces many women to lie about their true feelings regarding sex. Because women have been taught to view sex with romantic notions, they have difficulty dealing with it in terms of basic physical pleasure. To enjoy sex, be creative with sex, or initiate sex is to be a woman of "easy virtue."

She may have often used alcohol to lower her sexual inhibitions so that she could enjoy it. And if she did enjoy it, she could always deny it the next day by saying, ''I was drunk last night and I don't really remember much of what happened.'' It's all a way to protect her virtuous pedestal position.

Women need to explore the history of their sexual education and experiences in discussion groups with other women. They need to understand that a desire for sex is healthy, and that they are responsible for their own sexual pleasure in a relationship. This responsibility means that they must communicate their sexual needs to their partner without feeling embarrassed or guilty.

IV. Parenting Issues

Women with children experience guilt when they reflect on how their drinking affected their relationships. There is usually much denial in this area because the pain of failure is so intense. Culturally, motherhood is akin to sainthood. A good mother is a nutritionist, an educator, a playmate, a domestic, a loyal supporter of all the children's activities, a chauffeur, a nurse's aide, a good listener, and a consistent disciplinarian, to mention a few. The children must always come first.

This is another no-win situation for the female. If she deviates just a bit, she is trapped by guilt, believing that she is not a good mother. The alcoholic woman, because of the effects of the drug on her level of functioning, experiences this guilt even more intensely.

While in treatment, the woman needs to develop a more realistic view of herself as a mother. She needs to become aware of the unrealistic cultural expectations imposed on her. She must decide what kind of relationship she wants to have with her children—what kind of mother she wants to be.

She needs to appreciate her children as individuals and not as a major source of her self-esteem. She must learn to prepare them for responsible adulthood, and not as artifacts to demonstrate her ability to parent effectively. Because of her own inability to function equally in a relationship, she will find it difficult to respect her children as individuals, separate and apart from her. Due to her traditionally dependent position in relationships, she will encourage dependency from her children.

Once she develops a sense of her own self, feeling the freedom to be who she is, believing in her ability to take care of herself, she can allow her children to develop their own sense of self without feeling threatened. This requires an examination of her parenting history as well as a deeper understanding of her strengths.

If she is in an intact relationship, she must learn to involve her spouse in the rearing of the children. Once again, she must learn to communicate her expectations and needs to her spouse. In an alcoholic marriage, the male often assumes all major responsibilities. Upon returning home from treatment, the female must establish herself, both with her spouse and with her children, as an active member of the family unit.

V. Sex Role Conflict

Generally, sex role conflict refers to an inner struggle that a person may experience while trying to behave in stereotypical ways that are socially acceptable. For example, a woman is expected to be passive, dependent, non-competitive, and nurturing, whereas a male is expected to be aggressive, independent, tough, and competitive. A person's sex role identity is based on these traditional notions of what is ''male'' and what is ''female.''

Because of the upheaval in sex roles as a result of the women's movement, both men and women are somewhat confused about how they should act. Many women are especially distraught when faced with choosing between the traditional female role of homemaker, caretaker, and nurturer and the more recent career female role as competitor and aggressor.

Women need to learn about psychological androgyny, which is based on the assumption that an individual can be both masculine and feminine, blending these qualities into a balanced lifestyle which allows the freedom to choose rather than limiting behavior to outdated stereotypes. Both "masculine" and "feminine" traits are fundamental to the development of a healthy personality.

Groups in treatment should aim to help the female assess her sex role conflicts. If she rigidly adheres to what is expected, she will maintain the dependent, passive, powerless position that keeps her sick. In choosing new ways of behaving, ways that are not based on rigid stereotypes, she will achieve a more active and instrumental position in her environment. As a result, she will assume responsibility for her life and will feel that she has more control over her own destiny.

VI. Self-Esteem Issues

It goes without saying that if the woman deals with dependency and how she perpetuates dependent relationships, she will begin to function more actively in all aspects of her life. This will lead her to rebuild her self-esteem. Some treatment groups assist a patient in focusing on personal strengths by using verbal encouragement and praise. This is not enough. Treatment groups must help the woman begin to take responsibility for her life, for her recovery. This process begins with an assessment of her tendency to look for others to prop her up in life.

Treatment programs, if they are going to treat women, have a responsibility to provide lectures and therapy groups which will deal with recovery issues that are unique to the woman. Not only does this provide her with a relevant perspective, but the interaction in an all-female group gives her a sense of camaraderie and support that can never be experienced in a mixed group.

In a mixed group, women can hide behind their culturally imposed roles of compliance, nurturance, passivity, shyness, dependency, and manipulation through helplessness. Because of their own role expectations, men are prone to respond by being controlling, aggressive, powerful, and competitive. The issues the female patient needs to work out are then perpetuated in the dynamics of her own group therapy!

The purpose of this manual is to provide group treatment strategies. The exercises can be used in all-female groups where the veil of cultural expectations diminishes because women aren't as interested in fooling each other as they are in fooling those whom they perceive as having power. Time must be allotted in a core program for WOMEN ONLY groups. These groups must be mandatory and viewed by staff as an integral part of the core program. Staff attitude is critical to the success of such a program.

The strategies in this manual are intended to serve as springboards for discussion of some painful issues. There is no set sequence to their implementation; however, the women should meet at least twice a week to cover the treatment issues. These groups must be supplemented by individual counseling sessions and reading/writing assignments.

These strategies are not limited to a residential setting. Wherever a group of women come together for the purpose of recovery, these group experiences can be used. This includes aftercare groups, outpatient programs, or counseling groups in mental health centers.

Although these techniques were designed to be used in groups, they are useful in individual therapy with women. They provide an opportunity for therapist and patient to explore issues often avoided because of the female denial system.

The groups are easy to use and require only brief preparation time. One critical requirement for being a group leader is that the therapist first become aware of his or her own sexism and try to determine how he or she might perpetuate the myth of powerlessness during treatment. It is suggested, however, that a woman lead the groups.

STAFF TRAINING

No matter how aware one is about sexism in our culture, each of us is affected by cultural expectations. In order to implement an effective women's component to an existing program, it is essential that the treatment staff experience some consciousness-raising training groups. All the subtleties that perpetuate women's dependency and hinder a quality recovery process must be eliminated.

People often titter at all this fuss about women and their rights. They seem to think it's silly and deny there is a problem at all. This myopic attitude prevents women from reaching their full human potential. For alcoholic women, it prevents them from living life at all.

The following exercises are intended to aid the staff in realizing their own sex biases. They are to facilitate discussion around staff feelings and attitudes toward women.

I.   The entire staff should complete the exercise on sex roles in the manual (Chapter Three).

II.   Each staff member is to think of two or three key women in his or her life. On a sheet of paper, they are to list the adjectives that describe each woman.

The following questions can be used for discussion:

(1)   What are the predominant traits (male/female) of each woman?

(2)   How do you think this has influenced your expectations of women?

(3)   Which of the women do you remember most fondly? Why?

(4)   Which of the women do you remember most painfully? Why?

    (5)   How are the above memories related to stereotypical role models?

III.   Discuss as a staff if you think a woman should work or if she should stay at home and take care of husband and children. Members should share how their family of origin viewed the mother/wife. If there were siblings in the family, how were the girls treated regarding chores, career expectations, money, and dating compared to the boys?

IV.   Name your most respected woman in each of the following areas:
(1)   Politics
(2)   The arts
(3)   Education
(4)   Medicine/Science
(5)   Business/Industry
After her name, list the qualities that you admire most. How are these stereotypical? How are they not?

V.   What are the roles assumed in your current relationship? Who is the major nurturer, caretaker. Who is the major breadwinner? What determines these? Who is responsible for the management of finances? The management of the household upkeep? How are the tasks assigned between you and your spouse?

VI.   If you have children, what chores do you require them to do? List boys and girls separately. What activities do you encourage them to become involved in? What academic courses do you encourage them to pursue?

VII.   A group leader can clip highly charged pictures out of a magazine which portray women as sex symbols, victims of violence, or in any stereotyped role. These can be used to generate discussion in terms of reactions and feelings.

VIII.   Any provocative editorial dealing with a women's issue can be clipped and used for discussion.

CHAPTER ONE

Parenting

Rationale

This group is geared for women who have children. As women enter treatment, one of the most painful issues they have to face is how their drinking affected their ability to parent effectively. Rather than focus on failures, the purpose of this group is to help women plan and learn to use more effective disciplining techniques.

Objectives

1. To allow each woman the opportunity to share her feelings about her past parenting.
2. To allow each woman the opportunity to develop more effective techniques and strategies for re-entry into her family as a sober person.
3. To allow each woman the opportunity to gain support through role-playing with other group members.

Materials Needed

Chalkboard or newsprint and magic markers.

Group Activity

I.   Discuss how their chemical dependency interfered with their being an effective parent. Each participant should be encouraged to share her experiences.

    a.   Discuss with participants and list on the board which behaviors were *not* responsible (i.e., slapping children, not cooking, taking money for alcohol/drugs).

    b.   Discuss with participants which are more responsible behaviors (i.e., listening to the children, having dinner with them, taking them out for ice cream).

    c.   Emphasize that sobriety will give them the opportunity to function as responsible parents. Active chemical use interfered with their ability to parent and diminished their relationship with their children. Therapist should discuss this concept with the participants.

II. Another area that needs discussion is how *self-concept* affects the way a parent disciplines a child.

    a. Discuss GUILT and how this feeling often puts a parent in a position to compromise in order to make up for past shortcomings. This is especially true of the recovering woman.

    b. Children need rules and regulations. The term "discipline" is not limited to punishment. Children must be taught self-discipline and responsibility. They need assistance in learning to deal with the obligations and challenges of life. They must learn self-control. Discuss the need for structure and discipline and how permissiveness is a disaster for both parent and child.

    c. If a woman feels inadequate within herself, then any amount of rejection by a child will force her to give in, thus losing control. Point out that enforcing rules means that a parent must take a stand. Discuss.

    d. Discuss how attitude will influence behavior. An attitude of "I'll give her everything so she will forgive me," is nonproductive. If a woman returns home with excessive guilt, her parenting will be greatly affected. A more desirable attitude is "I have a responsibility to teach my child how to live effectively in this world. He or she is not my possession, but a person unique in his or her own right." Discuss.

III. Re-entry into family life will not be easy. Children will not know what to expect and will test the woman.

    a. Emphasize that a woman can't just go home and start making demands or imposing rules on the children. The children have been accustomed to very few restrictions.

The woman's sobriety is often viewed with anger by children because suddenly she is disciplining them. Discuss.

b. Discuss what rules would be reasonable to establish. Groups can be divided into TODDLER, ADOLESCENT, and PRE-PUBERTY. Areas to be considered can be: CHORES, ALLOWANCE, HOMEWORK, CURFEW, and GRADES, to mention a few. The concept of family meetings discussed by Virginia Satir in *Peoplemaking* should be covered as well. After discussing this concept, the therapist can break the group into three or four families. One person should be the mother and the others should be the children. Have them role-play their return home and how they would conduct a family meeting.

CHAPTER TWO

Feelings

Rationale

As a result of chemical abuse, the women have more than likely repressed many of their emotions and often simply detached themselves from their more painful feelings.
The first activity works quite well in a group setting while the second is very effective as an individual assignment to be discussed with the therapist on a one-to-one basis.

Objectives

1. To allow each woman the opportunity to experience feelings of joy, excitement, and happiness, as well as sadness, loss, and grief.
2. To allow each woman the opportunity to share these feelings with other women and experience group support.

Materials Needed

Sketchpads, watercolors, fingerpaints, paper.

Group Activity #1

I.   The therapist can prepare a brief presentation on feelings using Willard Gaylin's book *Feelings: Our Vital Signs*. This can be presented in a lecture format.
   a.   The therapist will give the following instructions: "Choose any art medium you wish. First, paint a scene representing the saddest and/or most painful time in your life. Please give some thought to this assignment. You have 25 minutes to do this, so use your time accordingly. Do not be concerned about your artistic ability. Just relax and draw."
   b.   When the time has elapsed, each person will stand up and be encouraged to discuss her scene. Was she drunk

or sober? Therapist should encourage her to share as much as possible.

c.   After all of the women have participated, the therapist should break for a few minutes, allowing the women to regroup their thoughts. After a ten or fifteen minute break, the women will be given the same instructions, only this time they are to paint a scene representing the happiest time in their life.

d.   Once again each person will stand up and share her scene.

II.   In a group setting, ask the women how they felt about the art therapy exercise. Discuss how powerful thoughts can be. Thinking about a happy time generally elicits happy feelings, and vice versa. Discuss how thoughts affect our feelings. Maxie Maultsby's book, *Helping Yourself to Happiness,* can be a helpful aid to this discussion.

Individual Activity
In an individual session, instruct the woman to develop a list of as many feelings as she can. Once she has completed this, she is to take each feeling and draw a picture which would best depict her conceptualization of it. Underneath each drawing she is to describe how this feeling sounds, and describe its physiological effects.

Example:
Fear
    The feeling sounds like a train whistle in the still of the night. The body feels cold, palms clammy and wet.
Anger
    The feeling sounds like thunder, loud and crashing. The body feels very tense, all muscles very tight, a burning knot in the stomach region.

After the woman completes the assignment, she can meet with her therapist and discuss each drawing. The therapist can use the material to delve into repressed and/or detached feeling states.

CHAPTER THREE
Sex Roles

Rationale

Culturally, men and women have been taught to behave in certain ways that are deemed appropriate for their sex. Men are expected to be more aggressive, dominating, and self-sufficient, while women are expected to be more nurturing, passive, and oriented toward others. Rigidly adhering to either stereotype is destructive to personal growth. Part of the stigma that women feel about their disease is a direct result of stereotypes such as "Nice girls don't get drunk." It is essential, therefore, that women begin to examine how stereotypes can keep them "sick." Androgyny is an attempt to destroy cultural expectations and to help individuals of both sexes have greater freedom in choosing behaviors and responses.

Objectives

1. To help each woman become aware of cultural stereotypes.
2. To help each woman recognize how adhering to these stereotypes constricts personality growth.
3. To help each woman learn the concept of androgyny.

Materials Needed

Magic markers, newsprint, copies of *Bem's Sex Role Inventory*. (See p. 21 for information on availability.)

Group Activity

I.   Distribute *Bem's Sex Role Inventory*. Give the participants a few moments to complete and collect.
II. Ask the women to discuss what adjectives come to mind in describing *MALE TRAITS*. The same is to be done for *FEMALE TRAITS*. List these traits on newsprint.
   a.   Discuss with the group what is generally expected of each sex. It will become quite obvious that the male

adjectives are extremely positive (i.e., independent, self-sufficient, provider, aggressive, strong) while the female adjectives are more negative (i.e., passive, nurturing, dependent, emotional, weak).

b. Discuss how the two are polarities and are actually extremes. Focus on how adhering too rigidly to either of these two extremes is constrictive to personality growth and development.

c. Discuss complementary/middle traits and how a blending of both the masculine and feminine allows the individual much greater freedom. Examples: If a man is sad, he can choose to cry without feeling embarrassment. If a woman wants to be ambitious or aggressive she can choose to do so without feeling like a "pushy bitch."

d. Introduce the concept of androgyny. DEFINITION: incorporating both masculine and feminine traits into one's personality, giving the individual much greater freedom to develop.

III. Return the *Bem Sex Role Inventory* and score. Have the women discuss their results. Have each woman share how she tends to be rigid in her own sexuality, adhering to what's expected of her by society's standards. Especially ask the following: What specific ways can you become more androgynous? How will androgynous behavior help you, especially in maintaining your sobriety?

IV. Refer back to the newsprint list of MALE and FEMALE TRAITS. As you review those adjectives which describe men, point out again how much more positive they seem than those adjectives used to describe women.

a. Ask the women if the following phrases are familiar: "I have more men friends than I do women friends."

"I get along so much better with men."
"I just don't trust women." Point out that, in making these statements, women are communicating a very clear message about themselves: "If you don't trust other women, then you obviously don't trust yourself." Discuss this concept with the women. Point out that, traditionally, men have been viewed as better than women. Having female friends is not seen as an asset. The therapist should encourage discussion of this issue.

b. Networking for women is a relatively new concept in the business world. It is crucial that recovering women form a networking system with each other. They must recognize that relationships with other recovering women are very important to their recovery. As they begin to develop these relationships, they will also begin to develop new feelings about themselves as women. *Recovering women need other recovering women.* Alcoholics Anonymous is based on the concept of sister- and brotherhood. Its success is contingent on camaraderie, a sharing of experiences. Women must see the value of developing a camaraderie with other recovering women. That is not to exclude relationships with recovering men, but it is important for the recovering woman to realize that she needs other recovering women. Discuss in depth.

Note: The *Bem Sex Role Inventory* can be ordered only from Consulting Psychologists Press, 577 College Ave., Palo Alto, CA 94306. Phone 415-857-1444.

CHAPTER FOUR

Real Self/Ideal Self

Rationale

All of us have some notion of who we are and who we would like to be. Psychologists refer to this psychic phenomenon as REAL SELF vs. IDEAL SELF. When a woman enters treatment, generally her perceptions of her real self and her ideal self are substantially distorted. In describing her real self, more than likely she will include images of her drinking self and tend to be her own worst enemy, which results in her viewing herself as despicable. In describing her ideal self, she will generally have images of perfection—unattainable and unrealistic characteristics. The result is DESPICABLE SELF vs. PERFECT SELF. As long as the female alcoholic continues to think of herself as either all BAD (DRUNK) or all GOOD (SOBER) she will continue to experience anxiety and depression, both during and after treatment.

Objectives

1. To help each woman creatively identify her "real" self-image.
2. To help each woman creatively identify her "ideal" self-image.
3. To help each woman recognize the discrepancy between the two, and how dangerous a large discrepancy can be to sobriety.
4. To help each woman develop a more realistic self-image.

Materials Needed

Clay, sketchpads, fingerpaints, watercolors.

Group Activity

I.   The therapist may prepare a brief lecture on real self vs. ideal self. Rubin's book entitled, *Compassion and Self-Hate,* and

DeRosis and Pellegrino's *The Book of Hope: How Women Can Overcome Depression,* can be used as resources.

II. Once this is completed, ask the group members to select a medium and give the following directions:
"The task at hand is to creatively depict your REAL SELF, that is, how you see yourself NOW. This can be in the form of an animate or inanimate object. Do not be concerned about its artistic merits. You have 25 minutes in which to complete this assignment. Afterwards, each woman will share her work with the group."
   a. After this is completed, ask each member to creatively depict her IDEAL SELF, that is, how she would like to be or wishes she could be.

III. The leader should ask questions which encourage exploration of the images. Focus on the characteristics of the sculpture or drawing that are consistent and realistic. Be especially cognizant of the discrepancies between the two images and those traits that are unrealistic.

IV. Discuss with the women how they think sobriety will facilitate the achievement of their ideal selves, and how chemical dependency will hinder it. The women will often have unrealistic expectations, hoping that sobriety will bring perfection. This must be discussed at length. Emphasize that sobriety brings normalcy, not perfection. Often in post-treatment therapy, women experience a real letdown because people aren't responding to them the way they want, or they aren't accomplishing things at the rate they feel they should be. Discussion should follow.

CHAPTER FIVE
Depressed States

Rationale

Statistics demonstrate that depression is a major problem for women. Due to the toxicity of the drugs ingested, the chemically dependent woman is even more susceptible to frequent periods of depression. She often feels that, once she abstains, these depressed states will no longer be a problem for her. Although there is some validity to this, depression will still affect her. Therefore, it is essential that women in treatment learn about depressed states and examine various strategies for coping with them.

Objectives

1. To help each woman learn about the four basic types of depression.
2. To help each woman explore the degree and frequency of her past depressed states.
3. To help each woman develop some specific strategies for effectively coping with her depressed states.
4. To help each woman recognize that she has some control over her depressed states.

Materials Needed

Chalkboard or newsprint.

Mini-lecture on Depression. Hand-out of incomplete sentences.

Group Activity #1

I.   Therapist may present a mini-lecture on depressed states using Wina Sturgeon's book, *Conquering Depression*. Include a brief definition of each of the following: clinical endogenous depression; reactive depression; toxic depression; psychotic depression.
II.   Distribute the incomplete sentences (See Appendix I) which deal with depressed states. This discussion is intended to be a warm-up for the following exercise.

Group Activity #2

I.   This activity allows the women an opportunity to examine depression in terms of feeling and behavior. As they begin to examine depression in light of its components, they will begin to feel as though they have more control over it. On newsprint the therapist will write the headings FEELINGS and BEHAVIOR. The group should then discuss and list first what they feel when depressed, i.e., worthless, angry, self-pity. Then they should discuss and list what they *do* when they are depressed, i.e., sleep, eat, stare into space. The therapist should point out the difference between feelings (internal states) and behavior (external states) and how our feelings affect our behavior and how the behavior continues to enhance the depressed feelings.

Example: **NEG. FEELINGS + NEG. BEHAV. = MORE NEG. FEELINGS**

| worthless | sleep | worthless |
| self-pity | drink | self-pity |

The therapist can then begin to focus on changing the negative behavioral response to a positive behavioral response. This can be accomplished by having the group discuss and list positive behavior which would replace the negative behavior.

Example: **NEG. FEELINGS   POS. BEHAVIOR**

| worthless | take a walk |
| self-pity | go to A.A. meeting |

The group should discuss how these positive behavioral responses will influence the negative feelings to become more positive.

Example: **NEG. FEELINGS   POS. BEHAV.   POS. FEELINGS**

| worthless | walk | more in control |
| self-pity | A.A. meeting | diversion |

The therapist can now move into a session in which the women would list what they think most often precipitates these depressed states. Generally, depression is due to a loss of something important such as a love bond. The elements include a feeling of rejection and a sense of not having met the expectations of others. The female learns relatively early in life to value herself only insofar as others value her. Her highest priorities are pleasing others, caring for others, being attractive for others. Her self-esteem is contingent upon the esteem of those around her. When she receives feedback from her environment that indicates that she has somehow failed, her most common response is depression.

Example:

PRECIPITATING FACT	NEG. FEEL.	POS. BEHAVIOR	POS. FEEL.
mother criticized me for drinking	worthless	call A.A. friend	in control
ruined dinner	failure	go out to eat	diversion self-for-give-ness

As the group discusses the precipitating factors, the therapist should focus on how these events imply that the woman has failed in the eyes of another or herself.

CHAPTER SIX

Dependence/Independence

Rationale

Culturally, women have been encouraged to be dependent on others for survival. This phenomenon has literally crippled women into believing that they are incapable of taking care of themselves. Feelings of powerlessness, helplessness, and hopelessness pervade the lives of many women. Alcoholic women are especially prone to intense feelings of inadequacy. Often their motive for entering treatment is to regain a relationship. Women in treatment must see how culturally ingrained dependency is an obstacle to their recovery.

Objectives

1. To help each woman learn the differences between dependence, independence, and interdependence.
2. To help each woman learn how she perpetuates dependent relationships.
3. To help each woman learn new ways of functioning in relationships.
4. To help each woman learn to assume responsibility for her own life and recovery.
5. To help each woman begin to get in touch with her own inner strength.

Materials Needed

Chalkboard. Newsprint and magic markers.

Group Activity

I.   The therapist may prepare a brief lecture on women's basic fear of independence using Colette Dowling's book, *The Cinderella Complex,* as a resource.

II. Ask the women to define the following terms:
     DEPENDENCE, INDEPENDENCE,
     INTERDEPENDENCE.
     Discuss in depth. Women often think being independent is
     not needing anyone. This is a distorted sense of
     independence. Discuss how they define a relationship
     (mutuality, caring, respect, supporting). What's the
     difference between support and being dependent? How can a
     woman be independent yet interdependent with another
     person?

III. Discuss how women are dependent upon others to get their
     self-esteem needs met. What are some other ways a woman
     can get these needs met? How does this kind of dependency
     create problems in a relationship?

IV. The women may do the following exercises as written
     assignments or as topics for group discussion.
     a. ''Now that I'm sober and I'm being a good girl,
         everyone should love me and take care of me.'' React to
         this statement and share your feelings.
     b. ''Who am I getting sober for? What happens when no
         one notices?'' React.
     c. ''How do I rely on others to give meaning to my life?''
     d. ''How can I become more self-sufficient in defining
         myself?''
     e. ''What do I expect from myself?''
     f. ''What, specifically do the following people expect from
         me?''
              husband   mother   in-laws
              boyfriend   children (each one)
              boss   father   friends
     g. Do you believe that you are capable and competent, able
         to be responsible for yourself? List some specific traits
         that indicate you are.

h. Imagine that you are alone in the world. There has been
    a nuclear attack and you are the sole survivor. All
    buildings are gone except for the library. Nature remains
    intact. Only human life has been destroyed. What would
    you do? How would you create a new life? How do you
    feel as you think about this fantasy?

CHAPTER SEVEN
Drinking Female Self/
Sober Female Self

Rationale

There is no doubt that alcoholism is a disease of denial. For the alcoholic woman this denial is especially strong because of the stigma that women face as "drunks." Treatment should aid women in coming to grips with their alcoholism and its effects on family and friends. The following exercise can be used effectively while women are in treatment. It can be an excellent tool to aid in breaking down denial, facing guilt feelings, and learning to be a responsible partner in relationships.

Objectives

1. To help each woman identify how she behaved while drinking and how this affected her self-image.
2. To help each woman identify how she behaved while sober and how this affected her self-image.
3. To help each woman separate behaviors from feelings.
4. To help each woman break down the denial surrounding her disease.

Materials Needed

Chalkboard. Newsprint and magic markers.

Group Activity #1

I.   The therapist will distribute two sheets of newsprint and give the women the following instructions:
     "You have 30 minutes in which to portray your DRINKING SELF. Remember, if you drank to the point of intoxication, your functioning was impaired. People experienced you drunk. What did they experience? Alcohol impaired your ability to function, not only at the task level (cleaning house, job, laundry), but also at the emotional level (isolation,

hostility). Be sure to include these areas as you complete this assignment. You may express this graphically or verbally.'' After the time is up, each woman is to share her drinking self with the group. The therapist should help the women focus on behaviors.

II. Once they have completed this, the discussion can center around how this drinking behavior affected others. Focus on behaviors and feelings. The therapist should point out that people are entitled to feel anger, hurt, and/or disappointment at another person's behavior. Internalizing these feelings and interpreting them as personal failures is irrational and non-productive.

Emphasize that the women must look at what they are doing: ''My drinking affects my behavior. I was drunk, therefore, I could not function properly. My family/boss/mother were angry and disappointed. They have a right to these feelings. What can I do about this situation?''

III. After this is completed, the women can then begin to focus on how their drinking made them feel about themselves. Emphasize that it's the behavior that they didn't like. They can change that by being sober.

IV. The next area for exploration is the SOBER SELF. Give the same directions as in exercise #1. Each woman will then share her sober self with the group. Women will often feel confused about this part of the assignment because they do not really know themselves as sober. Get them to think back to a time in their lives when they were sober and responsible. What were they like? What were they doing? How were they being responsible? Emphasis must be on behaviors. The therapist may even ask them to describe their sober self based upon their last few days of sobriety. What are they like since they have been in treatment? Perhaps the women can give each other some positive feedback to help one another realize that they have some real strengths as sober persons.

CHAPTER EIGHT

Relationships

Rationale

Being responsible to one's self first in sobriety is a concept which needs considerable attention for women in treatment. However, we do not live in a vacuum, and in addition to the necessities of food, clothing, and shelter, human beings need a sense of relatedness to other human beings. Treatment should aid the woman in coming to grips with her alcoholism and its effects on her significant others. She will return to an environment which will often not let her forget her past—at least not immediately. Therefore, it will prove helpful for her to deal with some of these unsolved relationship issues. Though she can't change the past, she must learn to live with it comfortably.

Objectives

1. To help each woman break down any residual denial about her disease.
2. To help each woman face how her drinking affected those closest to her.
3. To help each woman assess the status of her closest relationships.
4. To help each woman develop a plan of action to rebuild these relationships.

Materials Needed

Printed grids. (See Appendix II.)

Group Activity #1

I.   Distribute the grids to each woman and give the following instructions:
     "In this exercise you are to list on the grid how your drinking affected specific individuals in your closest

relationships. You have _____ (time) to complete this grid. Be prepared to return to the group and share the results.

II. Have each person share her grid, beginning with the person her drinking affected the least and moving to the person her drinking affected the most. The therapist should continue to stress behaviors and feelings as opposed to judgment and evaluation.

Group Activity #2

I. Following group activity #1, ask the women to develop a plan of action which will focus on rebuilding these relationships. Distribute the Personal Plan for Improving My Relationships (See Appendix III).

The women can be given a specific amount of time in which to complete the plan. They are then to return and share it in group. The therapist should make sure that they have listed specific *behaviors* in improving these relationships. Women sometimes tend to focus on *feelings* and will have difficulty recognizing their own power to take charge and create positive change in what appears to be a hopeless situation. Their tendency is to wait and let it happen to them. They may want something or someone outside themselves to carry the ball.

This exercise is intended to help them develop a plan of action which will give them a sense of power in creating healthy new relationships.

II. Another area that warrants some discussion is that of expectations. Ask the women to react to the following two statements:

"OK. I'm sober and I'm not drinking. See how good I'm being."

"OK. I'm sober and I'm not drinking, now you'll do what I want!"

Discuss the idea that their sobriety will bring them to normalcy. Women often think that sobriety will bring them happiness, perfection, love, etc. This only results in deep disappointment. Have the women discuss what they expect from their family members now that they are sober. The therapist should focus on what is realistic and what is not realistic.

CHAPTER NINE

The Five Boxes of Recovery

Rationale

Chemically dependent people tend to operate in extremes. The "All or None" theory is a major obstacle to maintaining a quality recovery. The women need to begin to plan for their post-treatment life. While they were drinking or consuming chemicals their main energies were expended maintaining their supply. Sobriety leaves a person with much free time, a real void in the day. Quality recovery is contingent upon achieving a sense of balance in one's life and with one's daily obligations. The purpose of this exercise is to help women work at reaching balance in their recovery.

Objectives

1. To help each woman develop a balanced post-treatment lifestyle.
2. To help each woman achieve a sense of power in her recovery and in the areas of daily living that she wants to work on.

Materials Needed

Printed sheets with the Five Boxes. (See Appendix IV.)

Group Activity

I. Discuss briefly how much of the women's time was consumed with their drugs. Emphasize that if one were to divide one's life into boxes: FAMILY, EMPLOYMENT, SELF-IMPROVEMENT, LEISURE, DRUGS, the women would discover that in the later stages of chemical dependency, most of their time was consumed within the box of DRUGS. Now that they are sober and working on their recovery, their life box of DRUGS would change into the life box of RECOVERY.

Emphasize that each and every life box needs some attention.
Distribute the Five Boxes sheet and ask the women to list
within each box what energy they plan to devote to it.

Example:

RECOVERY BOX:	A.A. meetings, aftercare meetings, therapy, spirituality, Alumni Group.
FAMILY BOX:	Sharing time with husband, children.
LEISURE BOX:	This includes those activities that give one pleasure, either alone or with family members, but you should include some leisure activity that you can do apart from family.
EMPLOYMENT:	This includes what you produce in terms of goods and services. If not a job, then perhaps maintaining your home, or volunteer work.
SELF-IMPROVEMENT:	This includes how you plan to work on your own growth through furthering your education, taking art classes, climbing a mountain, etc.

II.   After they complete the boxes, each woman can share with
the group or in pairs.
Emphasize that healthy recovery is such that the person
devotes energies to each area. Depending on current
lifestyle, the women may choose to put more energies into
one box than another. For example, now that they are
leaving treatment, they may wish to put more energy into the
RECOVERY box and less in the SELF-IMPROVEMENT

box. Stress that these boxes are fluid and can change every several months or so. Doing an inventory periodically will help the women work at maintaining energy levels in each area.

CHAPTER TEN
Identity Formation

Rationale

The purpose of this group activity is to raise the women's self-awareness about how they developed their self-image. More specifically, they will begin to differentiate those personal qualities which were "programmed" by society from those characteristics they willfully developed or will develop on their own. This will also aid them in feeling some power over their own destiny as recovering persons.

Objectives

1. To help each woman begin the process of self-definition.
2. To help each woman become aware of how much her self has been defined by the messages she received from others.
3. To help each woman willfully choose how she wishes to define herself at this point in her life.
4. To help each woman recognize the power she has in making choices for herself.

Materials Needed

Newsprint (four sheets for each woman) and magic markers.

Group Activity #1

I.   Distribute four sheets of newsprint and a magic marker to each woman and give the following instructions:
"At the top of one sheet of newsprint write the word GIRL in bold letters. At the top of the next one write the word ADOLESCENT. At the top of the next one write YOUNG ADULT, and on the last one write the word WOMAN."
Age limitations for each developmental stage can be determined by the group, although generally the following is acceptable: GIRL (0-11 years); ADOLESCENT (12-21 years); YOUNG ADULT (21-30 years); WOMAN (30 + years).

The therapist can then continue with the instructions:
"On each newsprint you are to write a string of words which best describe you at each stage of development. Traits can be repeated on several pages. Once this has been completed, decide through whom or under what circumstances you acquired the trait. You will then identify WHO or WHAT next to each trait on the newsprint.

Example:

GIRL	ADOLESCENT	YOUNG ADULT	WOMAN
loveable	secretive	impulsive	ambitious
(mother)	(mother)	(mother)	(boss)
spoiled	bright	secretive	selfish
(father)	(teacher)	(mother)	(mother)

III. Once the women have done this individually, they are to break into pairs or share their newsprint with the larger group. The therapist will ask the following questions to generate some discussion: Who gave you the most messages about yourself? How do you feel about that? Are these mainly positive or negative?

IV. The therapist should point out that much of how we perceive ourselves is based on feedback from others. We often let this feedback prevent us from growing or changing; we cling to antiquated notions about ourselves and generally dwell on our shortcomings rather than our strengths.

Group Activity #2

I. Instruct the women to move to a quiet place with their newsprint. In this part of the exercise they will work individually. They can tape the sheets to a wall where they can easily see the newsprint. Ask them to reflect on what they have written and answer the following questions on paper:

   1. What traits have remained constant throughout my life?

   2. Of these, which do I see as productive, as a strength? Which do I see as counterproductive, a weakness?

3. Which do I feel are accurate descriptions of me? Which are not?
4. Who has had the most input into my identity formation? How do I feel about this?
5. Which traits would I like to enhance? How can I do this? (Be specific and describe in behavioral terms.)
6. How do I feel about myself at this point in my life?

II. The women can then return to the group and share their responses.

CHAPTER ELEVEN

Who Am I?/Who
Would I Like to Be?

Rationale
This group can follow the IDENTITY FORMATION group. It will serve basically as a creative follow-up and reinforce the objectives of that group.

Objectives
To allow each woman the opportunity to creatively express her perceptions of her identity.

Materials Needed
Posterboard, scissors, paste, glue, magazines.

Group Activity

I. Distribute the materials and set a time limit for when the assignment will be due. The instructions are:
    "On one posterboard, creatively describe, through the use of magazines (collage), how you were as a GIRL, ADOLESCENT, YOUNG ADULT. Any pictures or slogans that depict you at that point in your development may be used. Once you have completed that assignment, complete a collage which would creatively depict you as WOMAN. This must include your drinking days as well as how you envision yourself as a recovering woman."

II. It usually takes several days for the women to complete this assignment. When a sufficient amount of time has elapsed, the group will reconvene and each woman must present her past self and her current self to the group.

III. The therapist should be especially observant of her WOMAN collage to see if she has included her drinking in the descriptions of herself. In addition, she should include A.A.

and aftercare in that part of her collage that depicts her recovering self. If these are slighted or omitted, a confrontation should take place in the group, as this may be an indication that she is still in a state of denial.

CHAPTER TWELVE

Parental Impact

Rationale

Discussing primary (early family) relationships with women in treatment can help them share feelings and conflicts that have long been ignored. Generally, women seem to have stronger attachment bonds to their primary families than do men. This group is intended to help women become aware of primary family dynamics and to help them assess these dynamics in terms of their effect on their current relationships.

Objectives

1. To help each woman gain an awareness of the dynamics of her early family relationships.
2. To help each woman gain an awareness of which relationship dynamics and characteristics she continues to use.
3. To help each woman gather additional data about herself.
4. To help each woman in her process of identity formation as a recovering, sober woman.

Materials Needed

Notebook paper, pencils.

Group Activity

I. Distribute paper and pencils to each woman and give the following directions:

"You are to divide your paper into four columns. At the top of each column you are to write:

MOTHER AS MOTHER   FATHER AS FATHER
MOTHER AS WIFE   FATHER AS HUSBAND

Now, list as many adjectives as you can which describe your parents in each of these roles as you perceived them.'' The therapist may talk briefly about roles and how we all function differently in some roles and the same in others. Examples can be given to demonstrate. MOTHER AS MOTHER could be *nurturing*, while MOTHER AS WIFE could be *cold*. The therapist can suggest some adjectives—cold, rejecting, timid, self-sacrificing, passive, self-conscious, weak, etc.

II.   The women should be given adequate group time to complete this assignment describing perceptions of mother and father. When they have finished, the therapist should instruct them as follows:

"Now I want you to circle any and all of those adjectives that also describe you. Be sure to circle *any* in all four columns." Once this is completed, go around to each participant and ask, "Who are you most like? How do you feel about that?"

III.   From this point on, the women should be allowed to freely discuss their reactions to this exercise. Generally, the women will have circled the most adjectives under the parent they have most identified with. If they like and/or respect this parent, there is generally no conflict. However, if they dislike the parent (which they usually do), there will be feelings of anger and hostility. Explore these feelings, as they give clues to self-esteem.

IV.   Next, the women need to focus on the relationship (Mother as Wife and Father as Husband) that existed between their parents. Have each woman describe her impressions of her parents' relationship. The therapist can ask, "What did you like about the relationship between your parents (its greatest strength)? What didn't you like (its greatest weakness)? How are your relationships similar? Dissimilar?"

V.   Move into a discussion of how their own relationships (past and present) may or may not have had similar dynamics. Distribute some sketchpads and waterpaints and have the women creatively depict the type of relationships they had while they were drinking. After a reasonable amount of time has elapsed, have each woman share her artwork and describe how she functioned in these relationships. Focus on how they were irresponsible.

VI. Instruct the women to take a sheet of paper and creatively depict the type of relationships they plan to be involved in as sober women. They should take each person (husband, lover, child #1, child #2, etc.) and describe specifically how they plan to be a responsible, functioning partner.

CHAPTER THIRTEEN
Sexuality: The Present

Rationale
It is important for women to recognize their sexuality as an important positive aspect of their humanity.
Objectives
1. To help each woman raise her awareness about her sexuality.
2. To help each woman discuss issues of concern around her sexuality.
3. To help each woman recognize that she has a responsibility to her own achievement of sexual satisfaction.
4. To help each woman develop the necessary assertive skills and apply them in her communication with her sexual partner.

Materials Needed
Sexuality: Incomplete Sentences. (Appendix V.)
Group Activity
I.   Present a mini-lecture on sexuality and intimacy. Focus on how drinking and chemical use is a major obstacle to achieving and maintaining a sexually satisfying and intimate relationship.
II.   Distribute the incomplete sentences list to the women, asking each person to complete it. When they have finished, they can volunteer to share their responses to any or all items on the list. This should be voluntary, considering the nature of the material, although each woman should be encouraged to participate.
III. Encourage the women to discuss their feelings about any of the items on the list. The purpose of this group is to serve primarily as an ice-breaker for further discussions on this issue.

CHAPTER FOURTEEN

Sexuality: The Past

Rationale

Sex is a topic that most people find difficult to discuss in a group. However, it is important that women in treatment be given an opportunity to discuss their sexual experience.

Objectives

1. To help each woman raise her awareness about her sexuality.
2. To help each woman discuss issues of concern related to her sexuality.
3. To help each woman recognize that she has a responsibility to her own achievement of sexual satisfaction.
4. To help each woman develop the necessary assertiveness skills and apply them in her communication with her sexual partner.

Materials Needed

Bowl and paper and pencils.

Group Activity

I.   Ask the women to write down on a piece of paper the following: (A prepared mimeographed copy of the following questions can be distributed.)
1. How old were you when you first learned about sex?
2. Where were you? What were you wearing?
3. Who told you?
4. How did you feel? What did you think about sex then?
Ask the women to voluntarily share the information with the group. The therapist should encourage interaction. This part of the group is intended to be an ice-breaker.

II. After this has been done, ask each woman to describe in writing her first sexual experience. She is to describe where, who, how old she was, and how she felt physically and emotionally, and how she decided to engage in sex.

After enough time has elapsed, each woman is to fold her paper in four and the therapist will pass a bowl around for each woman to place her experience into. Mix them up and have the first woman on the right select one experience (it can't be her own), read it out loud, and then share how she feels about this person's experience.

Example: "As I read this, I felt really sad that this person had to have her first encounter with a family member. It also makes me angry to think that her brother would do that to her. This would certainly affect me deeply and probably have an effect on my current ability to have sex."

Each woman is to select an experience and react to it. There is to be no discussion until after all experiences have been read. At this time the therapist may open the discussion by saying, "Let's talk about how you felt about this exercise." The remainder of the session should simply be discussion.

III.   Ask the women to write how this first experience affects their ability to function sexually today. After this is completed, ask them to voluntarily share their responses. The women should be encouraged to interact with one another and provide support.

IV.   Other discussion questions: How do I want my sex life to be now that I'm sober? What is my responsibility in achieving this goal? Do I really know my body well enough to know what "turns me on?"

The purpose of these questions is to help women recognize that they have a responsibility to their own sexuality. The therapist can present a lecture on assertiveness and sexuality. There are a number of excellent books on assertiveness that can be used as a resource.

CHAPTER FIFTEEN

Sexuality: Education

Rationale

Generally, women have very little knowledge about their own physiology, especially that which pertains to their sexual functioning. The purpose of this group is to present, in lecture form, the information regarding women and their bodies.

Objectives

1. To help each woman learn about her physiology as it pertains to her sexual functioning.
2. To allow each woman the opportunity to ask questions and to discuss her body and how it functions.

Materials Needed

Chalkboard, newsprint.

Group Activity

I.   Prepare a lecture on the female anatomy, especially as it pertains to sexual functioning and reproduction.
     The book *Our Bodies, Ourselves* can be an excellent resource. Disease which results from sexual contact should also be a part of the lecture.

II. The lecture should be followed by a question and answer period. The therapist can devise a list of questions (pre- and post-lecture) to see how much the women have grasped as a result of the lecture. Public libraries may be another resource, especially in audio-visual material.

APPENDIX I

Incomplete Sentences

1. My worst depression resulted from . . . .
2. When I'm depressed I'm . . . .
3. I'm usually depressed when I think about . . . .
4. Suicide is something I . . . .
5. Anyone who sees me when I'm depressed must think . . .
6. My depressions cause me to . . . .
7. I get depressed about every . . . .
8. The only positive thing depression does for me is . . . . . .
9. Depression is . . . .
10. I hate myself when . . . .

APPENDIX II

How Did My Drinking Affect the Following Significant Others?

WHO:	SPOUSE	CHILDREN	BOSS	FRIENDS	PARENTS
How did he or she treat me?	* verbally abusive * withdrew/ spent time at office	* ignored me * verbally abusive * resentful because they had to do chores * critical	* critical * resentful * treated me like child—always checking my work * condescending	* critical * withdrew/ made excuses not to see me	* denied any problem
How did I treat him, them, her?	* verbally abusive * in anger I threw things at him * cried * slept a lot	* verbally and physically abused * ignored them * blamed them for drinking	* sulked and pouted when she corrected me * slacked off on job * passive/ aggressive	* withdrew	* denial and withdrew
How did this impair the relationship?	* we both became angry & resentful * withdrew from one another * communication got really bad	* withdrew from one another * communication bad * developed distance	* resentment built up inside me	* dissolution of friendships * drinking was more important	* distance/lack of communication
Emotional dynamics	* anger * resentment * hate * cynicism * misery * loneliness * bitterness * rejection	* disappointment * resentment * frustration * pain * hurt * unloved * guilt	* frustration * resentment * guilt * worn-out * antagonistic * dissatisfied	* lonely * cynical * worthless * abandoned	* lonely * rejected * misunderstood * guilt * dissatisfied

* sample responses

APPENDIX III

My Personal Plan For Improving My Relationships

WHO	WHAT WILL I DO	EXPECTED BENEFIT
Husband - George	**SHORT RANGE BEHAVIORS** 1. * Conference while I'm here 2. * Determine what his resentments are 3. * Do two things alone on pass this weekend 4. * Tell him I'm sorry and that I love him 5. * Send him a funny card **LONG RANGE BEHAVIORS** 1. * Additional marriage therapy 2. * Take up golf together 3. * Be supportive of his Al-Anon involvement by asking questions about his meeting 4. * Go to one open meeting a month	* I believe these actions will bring us closer together and improve our communication * Nos. 1 and 4 will help me with my guilt * These actions should help us get to know one another again * To incorporate A.A. into our relationship
Becky - daughter	**SHORT RANGE BEHAVIORS** 1. * Spend 1 hour of Sunday pass with her alone 2. * Put my arm around her and tell her I love her 3. * Write her a letter of my amends **LONG RANGE BEHAVIORS** 1. * Go to three of her basketball games 2. * Go shopping for Prom dress 3. * Discuss her Alateen meetings 4. * Go out with her for dinner once a month	* These actions will begin to break down the resentments * These actions will get us involved with one another and will improve our communication and understanding of one another

* sample responses

APPENDIX IV

FAMILY

* week-end activities
  with children & spouse
  i.e., zoo, picnic

* dinner with spouse only
  three times a month

EMPLOYMENT

* part-time work at
  hospital (20 hrs.)
  3 days a week

RECOVERY

* aftercare groups weekly
* women's group on Friday
* lead meeting on Wednesday
* Big Book Readings
  daily

SELF-IMPROVEMENT

* art classes at university
* readings on assertiveness

LEISURE

* hot bath once a week
* meditation once a day

* sample responses

APPENDIX V

Sexuality: Incomplete Sentences

1. Sex is . . . .

2. My feelings about being sexually intimate are . . . .

3. Sex and drugs really . . . .

4. An orgasm is . . . .

5. When having sex, I . . . .

6. I like sex when . . . .

7. When I think of myself as a sexual being, I . . . .

8. My greatest fear about sex is . . . .

9. When I'm sober, sex . . . .

10. I don't like sex when . . . .

APPENDIX VI

Suggested Reading
For Patients

Many patients may feel a need to read more about their situation and the problems and joys they will encounter as recovering persons. The book list below includes the most recent publisher (usually paperback) to facilitate ordering, if so desired. Ideally, copies of these books should be on hand and readily available at the treatment center. This list should also be reproduced for each patient, to provide an additional resource for the future.

PARENTING AND DISCIPLINE
Dobson, James. *Dare to Discipline*. Bantam, 1977.
Dodson, Fitzhugh. *How to Discipline—With Love*. Signet, 1978.
Dodson, Fitzhugh. *How to Parent*. Signet, 1973.
Satir, Virginia. *Peoplemaking*. Science and Behavior Books, 1972.*

DEPRESSION
DeRosis, Helen and Pellegrino, Victoria. *The Book of Hope: How Women Can Overcome Depression*. Bantam, 1976.
Gaylin, Willard. *Feelings: Our Vital Signs*. Ballantine Books, 1979.
Maultsby, Maxie. *Help Yourself to Happiness*. Institute for Rational Living, 1975.
Rubin, Theodore. *Compassion and Self-Hate: An Alternative to Despair*. Ballantine Books, 1975.

FEMINIST AWARENESS
Alberti, Robert and Emmons, M. *Your Perfect Right*. Impact Publishers, 1978.*
DeBeauvoir, Simone. *The Second Sex*. Random House, 1974.
Dinnerstein, Dorothy. *The Mermaid and the Minotaur: Sexual Arrangements & Human Malaise*. Harper & Row, 1977.

Dowling, Colette. *The Cinderella Complex*. Summit Books, 1981.

Friday, Nancy. *My Mother, My Self: The Daughter's Search for Identity*. Dell, 1977.

Friedan, Betty. *The Feminine Mystique*. Dell, 1977.

Friedan, Betty. *The Second Stage*. Summit Books, 1981.

Gilligan, Carol. *In a Different Voice*. Harvard University Press, 1983.

Halcomb, Ruth. *Women Making It*. Ballantine Books, 1979.

Janeway, Elizabeth. *Man's World, Woman's Place*. Dell, 1972.

Millett, Kate. *Sexual Politics*. Avon, 1971.

Rich, Adrienne. *Of Woman Born: Motherhood as Experience & Institution*. Norton, 1976.

Schaef, Anne Wilson. *Women's Reality, An Emerging System in the White Male Society*. Winston, 1982.*

RELATIONSHIPS

Bach, George and Wyden, Peter. *The Intimate Enemy: How to Fight Fair in Love & Marriage*. Avon, 1981.

Beecher, Willard and Marguerite. *Beyond Success and Failure*. Simon and Shuster, 1966.

Ford, Edward and Englund, Steven. *Permanent Love*. Winston Press, 1979.

Ford, Edward and Zorn, Robert. *Why Be Lonely?* Argus Communications, 1975.

Satir, Virginia. *Making Contact*. Celestial Arts, 1976.

INSPIRATION

Anonymous. *Each Day A New Beginning*. Hazelden, 1982.*

Casey, Karen and Vanceburg, Martha. *The Promise of A New Day*. Hazelden, 1983.*

Cordes, Liane. *The Reflecting Pond*. Hazelden, 1981.*

Williams, Margery. *The Velveteen Rabbit*. Avon, 1982.

*Available through Hazelden Educational Materials, Box 176, Center City, Minnesota 55012. Phone 800-328-9000.

Female Alcoholism

Book References

Burtle, V. *Women Who Drink*. Springfield, IL: Charles C. Thomas.

"Medical and Psychological Aspects of the Drinking Patterns of Women Alcoholics." To be published as Chapter 2 in Burtle, V. ed., *Women Who Drink*. Springfield, IL: Charles C. Thomas.

Dalton, K. *The Premenstrual Syndrome*. Springfield, IL: Charles C. Thomas, 1964.

Estes, N. J., and Heenimann, N. E., eds. *Alcoholism: Developments, Consequences, and Interventions*. St. Louis: Masky, 1977, pp. 174-86.

Women with Alcohol Problems (Chapter 16 in N. J. Estes and N. E. Heenimann, eds. *Alcoholism: Development, Consequences, and Interventions*.) St. Louis, MO: Mosby, 1977, pp. 174-186.

Franks, V., and Burtle, V. *Women in Therapy*. Brunner/Mazel, New York: 1974, pp. 169-190.

Gomberg, E. S. and Franks, V. eds. *Gender and Disordered Behavior*. New York: Brunner/Mazel, 1978. Preface, Chapter: Problems with alcohol and other drugs, and Chapter: Reflections.

Greenblatt, M. and Schuckit, eds. *Alcoholism Problems in Women and Children*. New York: Grume and Stratton, 1976.

Hirsh, J. "Women and Alcoholism." In Bier, W. C., ed., *Problems in Addiction*. New York: Fordham University, 1962, pp. 108-115.

Hornick, E. L. *The Drinking Woman*. New York: Associated Press, 1977.

Kinsey, B. A. *The Female Alcoholic; A Social Psychological Study.* Springfield, 1966.

Kissing, B., and Begleiter, H. *The Biology of Alcoholism.* Planum: New York, 1976.

Korpman, B. *One Alcoholic Woman.* Washington: Linacre Press, 1948.

Schramm, C., Mandell, W., and Archer, J. *Workers Who Drink: Their Treatment in an Industrial Setting.* Lexington, Massachusetts: Heath, 1978.

Sherfey, M. J. "Psychopathology and Character Structure in Chronic Alcoholism." In: Diethelm, O., ed. *Etiology of Chronic Alcoholism;* pp. 16-42. Springfield, IL: Thomas; 1955.

Journal References

Angrist, S. S. "The study of sex roles." *Journal of Social Issues* 25: 215-232, 1969.

Beckman, L. J. "Self-esteem of women alcoholics." *Journal of Abnormal Psychology*, 1973, 82, 253-261.

Beckman, L. J. "Women alcoholics: a review of social and psychological studies." *Journal of Studies on Alcohol*, 1975, 36, 797-824.

Belfer, M. L., Shader, R. I., Carroll, M., and Harmantz, J. S. "Alcoholism in women." *Archives of General Psychiatry*, 1971, 25, 540-544.

Bem, S. L. "The measurement of psychological androgyny." *Journal of Consulting and Clinical Psychology*, 1974, 42, 155-62.

Bem, S. L. "On the utility of alternative procedures for assessing psychological androgyny." *Journal of Consulting and Clinical Psychology*, 1977, 45, 196.

Bem, S. L. "Sex-role adaptability: one consequence of psychological androgyny." *Journal of Personality and Social Psychology*, 1975, 31, 634-643.

Bem, S. L. and Lenney, E. "Sex-typing and the avoidance of cross-sex behavior." *Journal of Personality and Social Psychology*, 1976, 33, 48-54.

Benedek, T., and Rubinstein, B. "The correlations between ovarian activity and psychodynamic processes. I. The ovulative phase." *Psychosomatic Medicine*, 1939, 1, 240-270.

Block, J. H. "Conceptions of sex role: some cross-cultural and longitudinal perspectives." *American Psychologist*, 1973, 28, 512-526.

Broverman, I. K., Broverman, D. M., Clarkson, F. E., et al: "Sex role stereotypes and clinical judgments of mental health." *Journal of Consulting and Clinical Psychology,* 34, 1-7, 1970.

Browne-Mayers, A. N., Sulze, E. E., and Sillman, L. "Psychosocial study of hospitalized middle-class alcoholic women." *Annals of New York Academy of Sciences,* 1976, 273, 593-604.

Busch, H., Kormenday, E., and Feuerlein, W. "Partners of female alcoholics." *British Journal of Addictions,* 1971, 68, 179-184.

Charalampnes, K. D., Ford, B. K., and Sinner, T. J. "Self-esteem in alcoholics and non-alcoholics." *Quarterly Journal of Studies on Alcohol,* 1976, 37, 990-994.

Clarke, S. K. "Self-esteem in men and women alcoholics." *Quarterly Journal of Studies on Alcohol,* 1974, 35, 1380-1381.

Constantinople, A. "Masculinity-femininity: an exception to a famous dictum." *Psychological Bulletin,* 1974, 80, 389-407.

Corrigan, E. M., and Anderson, S. C. "Training for treatment of alcoholism in women." *Social Casework,* 1978, 59, 42-50.

Cramer, M. H., and Blacker, E. "Social class and drinking experience of female drunkenness offenders." *Journal of Health and Human Behavior,* 1966, 7, 276-283.

Curlee, J. "Alcoholic women: some considerations for further research." *Bulletin of the Menninger Clinic,* 1967, 31, 154-163.

Curlee, J. "Alcoholism and the 'empty nest.'" *Bulletin of the Menninger Clinic,* 1969, 33, 165-171.

Curlee, J. "A comparison of male and female patients at an alcoholism treatment center." *Journal of Psychology,* 1970, 74, 239-247.

Curlee, J. "Women alcoholics." *Federal Probation,* 1968, 32 (No. 1), 16-20.

Curran, F. J. "Personality studies in alcoholic women." *Journal of Nervous and Mental Disorders,* 1937, 86, 645-667.

Davis, C. N. "Early signs of alcoholism." *Journal of the American Medical Association,* 1977, 238, 161-162.

Deshaies, G. "Alcoholism of the female." *Revue de L'Alcoholisme,* 1963, 9, 235-247.

Dinaburg, D., Glick, I., and Feigenbaum, E. "Marital therapy of women alcoholics." *Journal of Studies on Alcohol,* 1977, 38 (No. 7).

Durand, D. E. "Effects of drinking on the power and affiliation needs of middle-aged females." *Journal of Health and Human Behavior,* 1961, 2, 283-292.

Fort, T. and Porterfield, A. L. "Some backgrounds and types of alcoholism among women." *Journal of Health and Human Behavior,* 1961, 2, 283-292.

Franck, L., and Rosen, E. "A projective test of masculinity-femininity." *Journal of Consulting Psychology,* 1949, 13, 247-256.

Fraser, J. "The female alcoholic." *Addictions,* 1973, 20, 64-80.

Galanter, M., Karasee, T. B., and Wilder, J. F. "Alcohol and drug abuse consultations in the general hospital: a systems approach." *American Journal of Psychiatry,* 1976, 133, 93-934.

Heilman, R. O. "Early recognition of alcoholism and other drug dependence." *Maryland State Medical Journal,* 1976, 25 (No. 19), 73-76.

Ivey, M. E., Bardwick, J. M. "Patterns of affective fluctuation in the menstrual cycle." *Psychosomatic Medicine,* 1968, 30, 336-345.

Jones, B., and Jones, M. "Alcohol effects in women during the menstrual cycle." *Annals of New York Academy of Sciences,* 1976, 273, 576-587.

Jones, B., and Jones, M. "Female intoxication doses or do women really get higher than men." *Alcohol Technical Reports,* 1976, 5 (No. 5), 11-14.

Jones, B., Jones, M., and Parades. "Oral contraception and ethanol metabolism." *Alcoholism Technical Reports, Oklahoma City,* 1976, 5, 28-32.

Keil, T. "Sex role variations and women's drinking." *Journal of Studies on Alcohol,* 1978, 39, 859-868.

Kinsey, B. A. "Psychological factors in alcoholic women from a state hospital sample." *American Journal of Psychiatry,* 124, 1463-1466, 1968.

Lindbeck, V. "The woman alcoholic — a review of the literature. *International Journal of the Addict,* 1972, 7 (No. 3), 567-587.

Lisansky, E. S. "Alcoholism in women; social and psychological concomitants." *Quarterly Journal of Studies on Alcohol,* 1957, 18, 588-623.

Lolli, G. "Alcoholism in women." *Connecticut Review on Alcoholism,* 1953, 5, 9-11.

Lynn, D. E. "A note on sex differences in the development of masculine and feminine identification." *Psychological Review,* 66, 126-135, 1959.

MacAndrew, C. "Women alcoholics: responses to scale 4 of the MMPI." *Journal of Studies on Alcohol,* 1978, 39, 1841-1854.

Medhus, A. "Conviction for drunkenness — a late symptom among female alcoholics." *Scandinavian Journal of Social Medicine,* Stockholm, 1975, 3, 23-27.

Megar, R. E., Wilson, W. M., and Helm, S. T. "Personality subtypes of male and female alcoholic partners." *International Journal of the Addictions,* 1970, 5, 99-113.

Morrissey, E., and Schuckit, M. A. "Stressful life events and alcoholic problems among women seen at a detoxification center." *Journal of Studies on Alcohol,* 1978, 39, 1559-1576.

Mulford, H. A. "Women and men problem drinkers." *Journal of Studies on Alcohol,* 1977, 38 (No. 9).

Noble, D. "Psychodynamics of alcoholism in a woman." *Psychiatry,* 1949, 12, 413-425.

Parker, F. B. "Sex role adjustment in women alcoholics." *Quarterly Journal of Studies on Alcohol,* 1972, 33, 647-657.

Parker, F. B. "Sex role adjustment and drinking disposition of women college students." *Student Alcohol Journal,* 1570-1573, 36, 1975.

Pattison, E. M. "Personality profiles of 50 alcoholic women." Abstract of paper preparation. University of California, Irvine, 1975.

Pitts, Jr., F. N., and Winokur, G. "Affective disorder VII Alcoholism and affective disorder." *Journal of Psychiatric Research,* August 1943, 4, 246-251.

Podolsky, E. "The woman alcoholic and premenstrual tension." *Journal of the Woman's American Medical Association,* 1963, 816-818.

Richards and Bascier. "Emotional stages in wives of alcoholics — during the descent and recovery process." *Journal of Alcohol and Drug Education,* winter 1978, 23, 12-17.

Rosenbaum, B. "Married women alcoholics at the Washingtonian Hospital." *Quarterly Journal of Studies on Alcohol,* March 1958, 19 (No. 1), 79-89.

Schuckit, M. A., and Grenderson, E. K. "Alcoholism in Navy and Marine Corps women: a first look." *Military Medicine,* 1975, 140, 268-271.

Schuckit, M. A., Pitts, F. N., Reich, T., King, L. J., and Winokur, G. "Alcoholism I. Two types of alcoholism in women." *Archives General Psychiatry,* 1969, 20, 301-306.

Schuckit, M. A. "The alcoholic woman. A literature review." *Psychiatry Medicine,* 1972, 3, 37-40.

Scida, J., and Vannicelli, M. "Sex role conflict and female drinking." *Journal of Studies on Alcohol.*

Scott, E. M., and Manaugh, T. S. "Femininity of alcoholic women's preferences on the Edwards Personal Preference Schedule." *Psychology Report,* 1976.

Sears, P. S. "Child-rearing factors related to playing of sex-typed roles." *American Psychologist,* 1953, 8, 431.

Seidan, A. "Research on the psychology of women I." *American Journal of Psychiatry,* October 10, 1976, 133, 1111.

Seidan, A. "Research on the psychology of women II." *American Journal of Psychiatry,* September, 1976, 133, 995.

Stafford, R. A., and Petway, J. M. "Stigmatization of men and women problem drinkers and their spouses." *Journal of Studies on Alcohol,* 1977, 38 (No. 11).

Symonds, A. "Neurotic dependency in successful women." *Journal of the American Academy of Psychoanalysis,* 1976, 4, 95-104.

Tamerin, J. S., Toler, A., and Harrington, B. "Sexual differences in alcohol a comparison of male and female alcoholics, self and spouse perceptions." *American Journal of Drug and Alcohol Abuse,* 1976, 3, 457-472.

Tiebout, H. M. "The act of surrender in the therapeutic process." *Quarterly Journal of Studies on Alcohol,* 1949, 10, 48-58.

Tiebout, H. M. "The ego factors in surrender in alcoholism." *Quarterly Journal of Studies on Alcohol,* 1954, 15, 610-621.

Van Amberg, R. J. "A study of 50 women patients hospitalized for alcohol addiction." *Disorders of the Nervous System,* 1945, 4, 246-251.

Wall, J. H. "A study of alcoholism in women." *American Journal of Psychiatry,* 1937, 93, 943-952.

Warner, R. H., and Rosett, H. L. "The effects of drinking on offspring: an historical survey of the American and British Literature." *Journal of Studies on Alcohol,* November 1975, 36, 1395-1420.

Watson, G. and Lawson, D. M. "Effects of alcohol on sexual arousal in women." *Journal of Abnormal Psychology,* 1976, 85, 489-497.

Wilsnack, S. C. "The effects of social drinking on woman's fantasy." *Journal of Personality,* March 1974, 42 (No. 1), 43-61.

Wilsnack, S. C. "Femininity by the bottle." *Psychology Today,* April 1973, 6 (No. 11), 39-43.

Wilsnack, S. C. "Sex role identity in female alcoholism." *Journal of Abnormal Psychology,* 1973, 82, 253-261.

Wilsnack, S. C. and Wilsnack, R. "Sex roles and drinking among adolescent girls." *Journal of Studies on Alcohol,* 1978, 39, 1855-1873.

Winchester. "Special problems of women alcoholics." *Reader's Digest,* March 1978, 112, 207-208.

Winokur, G., and Clayton, P. "Family history studies: II. Sex differences and alcoholism in primary affective illness." *British Journal of Psychiatry,* September 1967, 114, 973-979.

Wood, H. P., and Duffer, E. L. "Psychological factors in alcoholic women." *American Journal of Psychiatry,* 1966, 123, 341-345.

Wright, B. V., and Taska, S. "The nature and origin of feeling feminine." *British Journal of Social Clinical Psychology.* Psychol. 5, 140-149, 1966.

Zellen, S., et al. "Sex contingent differences between male and female alcoholics." *Journal of Clinical Psychology,* 1966, 22, 160-165.

Other titles that will interest you...

Each Day a New Beginning
For women, sometimes recovery can seem like a huge puzzle with lots of pieces. Each piece of the puzzle is an integral part of the larger picture of ourselves in recovery. Here is a daily meditation book that considers these many pieces and their relationship to recovery. Each day we have opportunities to actualize our goals, our hopes and our dreams. This book can empower us, and each day can truly be a new beginning. (400 pp.)
Order No. 1076

Women's Issues
by Kathleen Rowe
Combining A.A. philosophy, women's experiences, and ideas for group support, this new booklet presents a problem-solving, self-actualizing approach to thirteen common issues for recovering women today. (40 pp.)
Order No. 5498

Women and Relapse
by Suzanne Boylston Cusack, C.A.C.
The author suggests the causes for relapse among women are often related to social roles and attitudes. Citing actual case histories, Cusack suggests ways to help such women. (36 pp.)
Order No. 1379
